If you Whistle at a Thistle

If you whistle at a thistle
It'll turn its head.
If you compliment a carrot
It'll turn bright red.

If you squeeze a pickled onion
It'll start to cry.
If you cuddle a fresh cabbage
It'll softly sigh.

Never Take a Bath in the Dark

Compiled by Catherine Baker

Illustrated by Olga Demidova, Robin Boyden,
Mark Long, Dan Bramall, Meg Hunt, Leo Broadley, Daron Parton,
Agnese Baruzzi, Mark Beech, Laura Ellen Anderson,
Sole Otero and Yannick Robert

Contents

If you tickle a dill pickle
It'll give a girlish giggle.
If you stroke an artichoke
It'll squirm and wriggle.

If you caress a bunch of cress
It'll go quite weak.
But if you try to kiss a turnip
It'll slap you on the cheek.

John Foster

Meeting on a Plate

A snail met a worm
on a lettuce leaf
in a plateful of salad
one day.

They agreed
that the world
is a wonderful place;
'So green,'
said the worm.
'So cool,'
said the snail
as they nibbled
a cucumber slice.

They slid
along celery,
tasted tomatoes;
'So soft,'
said the snail.
'So wet,'
said the worm,
and they travelled
a watercress stalk,
happily talking,
until up above them
somebody lifted
a big knife and fork.

Irene Rawnsley

8

The Schoolboy of Rye

There was a young schoolboy of Rye,
Who was baked by mistake in a pie.
To his mother's disgust,
He emerged through the crust,
And exclaimed, with a yawn, 'Where am I?'

Anon

Waiter, waiter, will my pizza be long?

No, sir. It will be round.

Doctor, doctor. Every time I drink coffee
I get a stabbing pain in my right eye.

Next time, take the spoon out of the cup first.

Fruit Fantasy

They say that what you eat

is what you are

so if I eat a star fruit

will I be a star?

If I eat a dragon fruit

will I start breathing fire?

If I eat a kiwi

will I become a flier?

If I eat a papaya

will I become my dad?

If I eat bananas

will I go raving mad?

If I eat a prickly pear

will I split into two?

And if I eat an ugli fruit

will I look like you?

Alan Durant

Elastic Jones

Elastic Jones had rubber bones.
He could bounce up and down like a ball.
When he was six, one of his tricks
Was jumping a ten-foot wall.

As the years went by, Elastic would try
To jump higher, and higher, and higher.
He amazed people by jumping a steeple
Though he scratched his behind on the spire.

But, like many a star, he went too far,
Getting carried away with his power.
He boasted one day, 'Get out of my way,
I'm going to jump Blackpool Tower.'

He took off from near the end of the pier,
But he slipped and crashed into the top.
Amid cries and groans, Elastic Jones
Fell into the sea with a plop.

John Foster

The Kleptomaniac

Beware the Kleptomaniac
Who knows not wrong from right

He'll wait until you turn your back
Then steal everything in sight

The nose from a snowman
(Be it carrot or coal)

The stick from a blind man
From the beggar his bowl

The smoke from a chimney
The leaves from a tree

A kitten's miaow
(Pretty mean, you'll agree)

He'll pinch a used tea bag
From out of the pot

A field of potatoes
And scoff the whole lot

(Is baby still there
Asleep in its cot?)

He'll rob the baton
From a conductor on stage

All the books from the library
Page by page

He'll snaffle your shadow
As you bask in the sun

Pilfer the currants
From out of your bun

He'll lift the wind
Right out of your sails

Hold your hand
And make off with your nails.

When he's around
Things just disappear

F nnily eno gh I th nk
Th re's one ar und here!

Roger McGough

Bubblegum Pete

This is the story of Bubblegum Pete
Who ate all the bubblegum he could eat.
There was gum in his pockets and gum in his boots,
Gum in his socks and his shorts and his suits.

Sticky pink lumps, sometimes wrapped, often not,
Wherever he went to, the bubblegum got.
And when he had finished this mess of a sweet,
He would spit it and stick it on somebody's seat.

'Please don't chew gum, you are sure to get wind,'
His mother asked kindly, but Peter just grinned.
But wind as it happened did give him some trouble
When Pete blew the world's biggest bubblegum bubble.

He was out in the garden with nothing to do
So he put in some gum and he started to chew.
When it went mushy he started to blow
And little by little it started to grow.

As big as a golf ball, as big as a mouse,
As big as a horse then as big as a house.
The giant gum bubble was caught by a breeze
Which wafted poor Peter up over the trees.

Higher and higher right over the steeple,
Higher until he could not see the people,
Up in the clouds like some rare sort of bird,
Where silly boys crying for help can't be heard.

Higher than spaceships and higher than stars,
Higher than Venus and Saturn and Mars.
'I will never blow bubbles again. I will stop,'
Said Peter quite rightly. The bubble went

POP!

Jeanne Willis

By Comparison

Claire's debonair, but Amanda is grander.

Daisy is lazy, but Jean's very keen.

Heidi's untidy, but Marguerite's neat.

Bertie is dirty, but Nadine is unclean.

Frankie is swanky, but Shaun is withdrawn.

Solly is jolly, but Brad's very sad.

Hannah's got manners, but Ruth is uncouth.

Pattie is batty and Maddie's quite mad.

Connie is bonny, but Jane's very plain.

Ted is well-bred, but Jude's very crude.

Lester's a jester but Dave's very grave.

Billy's just silly, but Gertrude is rude.

John Foster

The Ostrich

The ostrich roams the great Sahara,
Its mouth is wide and narra.
It has such long and lofty legs,
I'm glad it sits to lay its eggs.

Ogden Nash

What do you give a sick frog?

A hoperation!

What type of lion can you find in your back garden?

A dandelion!

What do you call a sheep with no legs?

A cloud!

Guinevere

Guinevere, the tabby cat,
Goes to school in her little hat.
She walks along with a little mouse
That she eats for lunch.

Vivienne Howells

I Found a Little Puppy

I found a little puppy dog,
His coat was soft and brown.
He had two beady little eyes
That looked me up and down.
He had a funny little tail.
I found him in a drain,
But Mother wasn't too impressed
And put him back again.
She screamed, 'He is no puppy,
I am very sure of that!'
But I am sure she'll grow to love
My little sewer rat.

Jeanne Willis

The Umbrella Bird

The umbrella bird is known to live
In Ecuador and Peru,
With several aunts and uncles
In Brazil and Chile too.

It often rains in those parts,
Which suits them without doubt
For unless it's raining quite a lot
The umbrella bird won't come out.

Martin Honeysett

Electric Advice

Never take
A bath in the dark.
You might use the wrong flannel
or sit on a shark.

Adrian Mitchell

25

The Peruvian Llama

An extraordinary beast is the llama.

Almost oval, yet oblong and square,

Not a fish, nor a fowl,

Neither fruit bat nor owl,

And its coat's not quite wool, not quite hair.

An unusual beast is the llama,

The Peruvians cherish it most:

For they feed it on chocs

And then herd it (in flocks)

From the Andes right down to the coast.

A remarkable beast is the llama,

And its habits are skittish and quaint;

When they shave off its fleece,

The poor llama says: 'Please

Won't you give me a new coat of paint?'

An impossible beast is the llama,

Like a goat but with much longer legs,

And a hairy great snout

Which it turns inside out

As it drops to its knees and begs:

'I'm a sad little beast I'm a llama;
And it hurts when I'm prodded or poked,
For it truly upsets me
When my master forgets me;
It's a blessing I'm hard to provoke!'

An unfortunate beast is the llama,
Neither elegant, charming nor cute;
If its life isn't full
As a grower of wool,
Can we ever console the poor brute?

Christopher Mann

The early bird gets the worm - but the second mouse gets the cheese!

Sheep are baaaaad drivers!

Pete's Pets

Special offer today!
Hamsters from Hamsterdam

Hickory Dickory Dock ➡

Never Forget the Birthday of Anyone who has Antlers Bigger than your Body

No excuse

Is any use

To a deeply offended moose

Adrian Mitchell

Eileen Idle

Eileen Idle's eyebrows,
The hairiest of features,
Make the perfect hiding place
For shy little creatures.

Deep in Eileen's eyebrows,
Field mice meet for talks,
And wrens enjoy a game of cards
Safe from sparrowhawks.

Richard Edwards

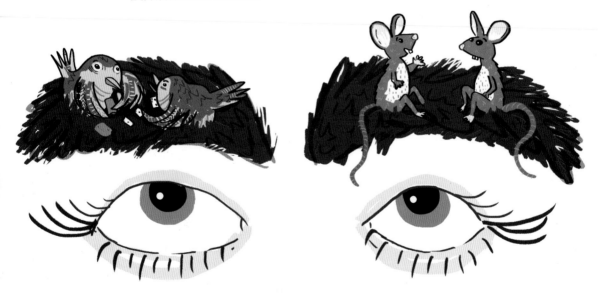

Mascot

Watching my local football team play
Would definitely be more fun
If the other team managed fewer goals
And our team occasionally won.

And I'd certainly enjoy it better if
I was taller than four foot three
So that when we managed not to score
At least I'd be able to see.

And I wish our penguin mascot
Wouldn't act so stupid and sad
And keep his head on till we get home
So no one would know it's my dad.

Gareth Owen

Why didn't the two elephants want to go swimming?

They only had one pair of trunks between them.

Why was Cinderella no good at football?

Her coach was a pumpkin.

Why was the football pitch shaped like a triangle?

Somebody took a corner.

Why did the basketball court get wet?

The players dribbled all over it.

A Good Idea

Today I might just make
one of my inventions.
What will you invent?

A machine to stand by the cooker
and stir the gravy.
Mum can have time off.
But who will do the vegetables?

This machine has another arm
which can peel potatoes,
chop them up
and put them in the pan.
But who will buy the potatoes?

This machine has another arm
with a basket on the end
which stretches out of the door,
down the street
and into the greengrocer's shop.
But how does it pay the shopkeeper?

You put money in the basket,
he puts in potatoes.
But what if someone steals the money?

This machine has another arm
with a policeman on the end,
carrying a truncheon.

Will it be ready by dinner time?

No. Today I might just help Mum
to make the dinner myself.

Irene Rawnsley

Chicken Poxed

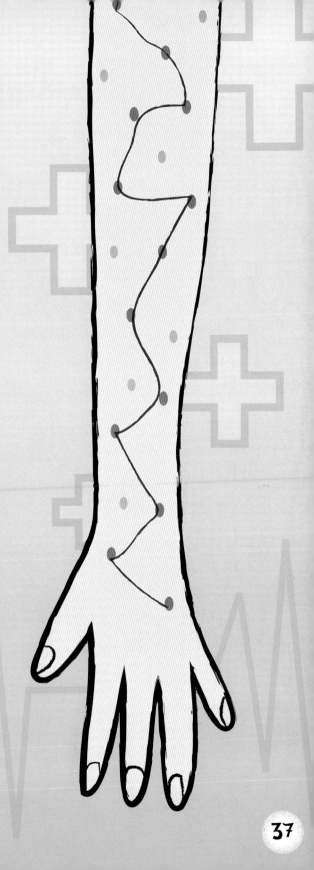

My sister was spotty,
Real spotty all over,
She was plastered with spots
From her head to her toes.

She had spots on the parts
That her bathing suits cover,
Spots on her eyelids,
Spots on her nose.

I didn't know chickenpox
Could be so interesting,
It seemed such a shame
To waste all those spots.

So when Jody was sleeping
And no one was looking,
I got a blue pen
And connected her dots.

Valerie Bloom

My Mum Says

My mum says:
If you don't pick up your pyjamas
And fold them under your pillow,
I'll throw them out of the window
For the binmen to pick up.

If you don't go upstairs
And get washed immediately,
I'll take you out into the garden
And turn the hosepipe on you.

If you don't hurry up
And get dressed at once,
I'll take you to school
In your knickers.

If you're not out of this door
In ten seconds' time,
I'll kiss you goodbye outside school.

My mum says:
You think I'm joking, don't you?

John Foster

Loopy Limericks

There once was a girl who said, 'Why
Can't I look in my ear with my eye?
If I put my mind to it,
I'm sure I can do it.
You never can tell till you try.'

Anonymous

There once was a young girl called Maggie
Whose dog was enormous and shaggy.
The front end of him
Was vicious and grim
But the tail end was friendly and waggy!

Anonymous

There was an Old Man with a beard,
Who said, 'It is just as I feared! —
Two Owls and a Hen,
Four Larks and a Wren,
Have all built their nests in my beard!'

Edward Lear

Christmas Thank Yous

Dear Auntie
Oh, what a nice jumper
I've always adored powder blue
And fancy you thinking of
orange and pink for the stripes
How clever of you.

Dear Uncle
The soap is terrific
So useful and such a kind thought
And how did you guess
that I'd just used the last
of the soap that last Christmas brought?

Dear Gran
Many thanks for the hankies
Now I really can't wait for the flu
And the daisies embroidered
in red round the 'M' for Michael
How thoughtful of you.

Dear Cousin

What socks!

And the same sort you wear

so you must be the last word in style

And I'm certain you're right that the luminous green

will make me stand out a mile.

Dear Sister

I quite understand your concern

It's a risk sending jam in the post

But I think I've pulled out all the big bits of glass

so it won't taste too sharp spread on toast.

Dear Grandad

Don't fret – I'm delighted

So don't think your gift will offend

I'm not at all hurt

that you gave up this year

and just sent me a fiver to spend.

Mick Gowar

Dad's Got a Ukulele

Dad's got a ukulele
He's ukulele mad
He plays and plays it daily
My ukulele dad.

He's ukulele bonkers
He's happy and he's glad
My grinning, humming, finger-strumming
ukulele dad.

Paul Cookson

Batty Books

Babysitting by Justin Casey Howells

Daddy, Are We There Yet? by Miles Away

End of the Week by Gladys Friday

COME ON IN BY DORIS OPEN

The Haunted House by Hugo First

You're a Big Boy Now by Tyrone Laces

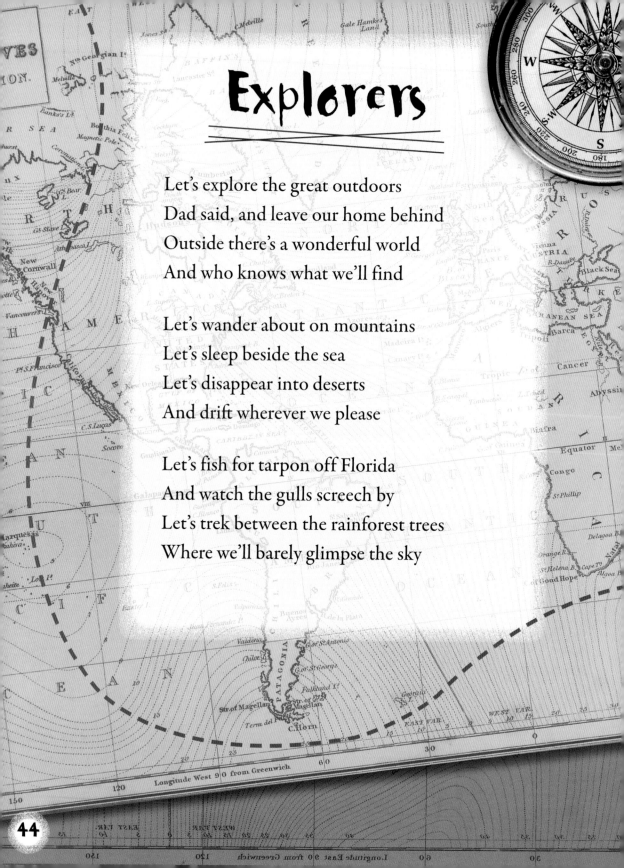

Explorers

Let's explore the great outdoors
Dad said, and leave our home behind
Outside there's a wonderful world
And who knows what we'll find

Let's wander about on mountains
Let's sleep beside the sea
Let's disappear into deserts
And drift wherever we please

Let's fish for tarpon off Florida
And watch the gulls screech by
Let's trek between the rainforest trees
Where we'll barely glimpse the sky

We'll carry our home on our backs
We'll camp by rivers and streams
By day we'll follow railroad tracks
By night we'll follow our dreams

And we won't take the easy option
We'll laugh when the going gets hard
But just for tonight we'll both play safe
And camp in our back yard

Brian Moses

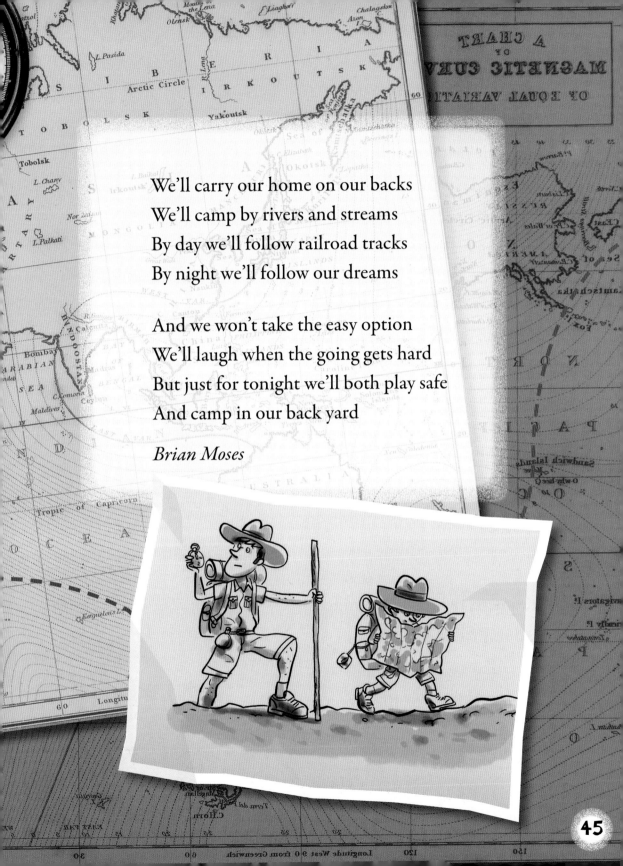

My Uncle's Wedding

My uncle married a monkey
We called her Aunt Baboon,
We all went to their wedding
In the merry month of June.

The bridesmaid was a gibbon,
The page boy was a goat,
The best man a gorilla who
Got Grandpa by the throat.

The vicar was a rhino
And this was a mistake;
He charged the congregation and
He tossed the wedding cake.

The guests behaved like animals
And trashed the hotel room,
But sad to say the worst behaved
Was Uncle George, the groom.

Jeanne Willis

Why was the little strawberry crying?

Because his parents were in a jam.

Knock knock.

Who's there?

Canoe.

Canoe who?

Canoe help me with my homework please, Dad – I'm stuck!

What did the hedgehog say to the cactus?

Is that you, Mum?

About Catherine Baker

I've always loved funny poems and
jokes (who doesn't?) and I had a great
time putting this anthology together. The only
tricky bit was that I did most of my research in a library.
Libraries are meant to be calm, peaceful places, but I must
have broken the 'no loud giggling, chortling or guffawing'
rule a million times. (It's a good thing they don't have a
'no exaggerating' rule!)

One of my favourite poets is Adrian Mitchell and I did
want to call this anthology 'Never Forget the Birthday of
Anyone who has Antlers Bigger than your Body', because
that's the best piece of advice I've ever had from a poem.
It wouldn't fit on the cover, though. Shame.